A Walker's
WIRRAL SHORE WAY
Chester to Hoylake

Carl Rogers

Mara Publications

Published in March 1994 by Mara Publications, 22 Crosland Terrace, Helsby, Warrington, Cheshire.

All enquiries regarding sales - tel: (0928) 723744.

ISBN 0 9522409 0 4

British Library Cataloguing-in-publication data.
A catalogue for this book is available from the British Library.

Whilst every effort has been made to ensure that the information in this book is correct, the author or the publisher can accept no responsibility for errors, loss or injury however caused.

Text, maps and cover photograph copyright Carl Rogers 1993.

Illustrations by Roger Oldham taken from "Picturesque Cheshire" by T. A. Coward, published by Sherratt and Hughes in 1903.

Maps based on the Ordnance Survey 1:25,000 map with the permission of the controller of H.M. Stationary Office. Crown Copyright.

Contents

	page
Introduction	4
1. Blacon - Shotwick 4 3/4 miles	6
2. Shotwick - Parkgate 6 miles.	12
3. Parkgate - Thurstaston Common 5 1/2 miles	20
4. Thurstaston Common - Hilbre Point 4 1/2 miles	26

Cover photograph: Hilbre from Middle Eye.

Introduction

The *Wirral Shore Way* is a long distance footpath which runs along the western side of the Wirral peninsula keeping as close as possible to the old coastline. Although it is not a coastal walk (the coast is not continuously accessible to the public), the coast is very much its theme and en-route you will visit many relics from Wirral's maritime past.

For over 1,000 years Chester lay at the head of a major estuary whose waters brought shipping right up to the city walls. This enabled it to develop as a substantial sea port before shallowing of the estuary in the Middle Ages brought problems. Unlike the Mersey, the wide estuary of the Dee is unable to sweep itself clear of sands and thus a relentless siltation of the river began. As a result, a succession of anchorages and smaller ports were established along Wirral's western coast culminating in Parkgate, perhaps the most famous of all and one of the last to be abandoned.

Relics of these activities are still to be seen and you will be able to trace the old coastline, now far inland, at several locations. In addition there are castle remains, ancient salt roads and islands where a Dark Age hermit lived out her solitary existence.

The *Wirral Shore Way* is not just an historic trail, it is extremely varied and will take you through some of Wirral's finest countryside, from picturesque villages and quiet country lanes to exposed hilltops and sandy beaches.

The gentle terrain (even on the hilly sections) is suitable for walkers of all abilities and can be enjoyed at any time of year. At a little over 20 miles, it is possible to complete in a single day, but if you feel this is too much, or, that you would rather tackle it at a more leisurely pace, the route description has been divided into four shorter sections.

Refreshments
The *Wirral Shore Way* passes through several villages and refreshments are readily available at local shops, pubs and cafes.

Public Transport
Public transport can be used to reach either end of the route. Trains can be taken from West Kirby to Chester changing at Hamilton Square and Hooton. Alternatively, Crosville operate the C22 service which calls at several villages along the route such as Heswall, Parkgate, Puddington, Burton and Saughall. Consult local timetables for specific times.

Maps
Although this booklet contains all the information you will need to find your way, it is a good idea to take along copies of the relevant Ordnance Survey Landranger maps for an over view of the whole route and to identify additional features along the way. Sheet numbers are given below.

The sketch maps which accompany the text are based on the Ordnance Survey Pathfinder maps which have a larger scale and are excellent for walking. These show every field boundary and building, and are overprinted with public rights of way information. Sheet numbers for these maps are given below.

Ordnance Survey Landranger 1:50,000;
sheets 108 Liverpool and 117 Chester and Wrexham.

Ordnance Survey Pathfinder 1:25,000 ;
sheets 738 756 and 773.

Chapter 1
Blacon - Shotwick
Distance 4 3/4 miles

Start
Begin at the junction of Saughall Road and Saxon Way in Blacon where a green lane, known as Kingswood Lane, cuts through fields towards Saughall village. Grid ref. 379 686 (Landranger 117).

The Route
The first mile or so of our route follows Kingswood Lane, an important highway in past centuries but now almost forgotten. It originally led from Chester to the royal woods at Shotwick Park before continuing to Shotwick village. Earlier still it was known as "Saltsway" indicating the existence of an ancient salt merchants route on this side of Wirral during the Middle Ages. A millennium earlier Roman legionaries may well have marched this way en-route to their outpost at Meols.

1. Follow Kingswood Lane for about one mile. Immediately beyond the second group of buildings on the left, turn left into fields. Bear half-left through the centre of the field to a well hidden stile in the bottom corner. Cut through the centre of the next two fields following a line of stiles before bearing left around the field edge in the third field. A stile and short entry now lead into a housing estate. Turn right at the road (The Riddings) and continue for some distance to a T junction. Turn left here and after about 40 yards bear right into Darlington Crescent. Look for Smithy Close, a short cul-de-sac on the left with a footpath at its head leading to Church Road.

Although Great Saughall is an ancient village it seems to have few tales to tell. It was not named among the Dee ports which line the old coastline further north, although the tide came to within half a mile of our present location until the reclamation schemes of the eighteenth century transformed much of the River Dee into farmland.

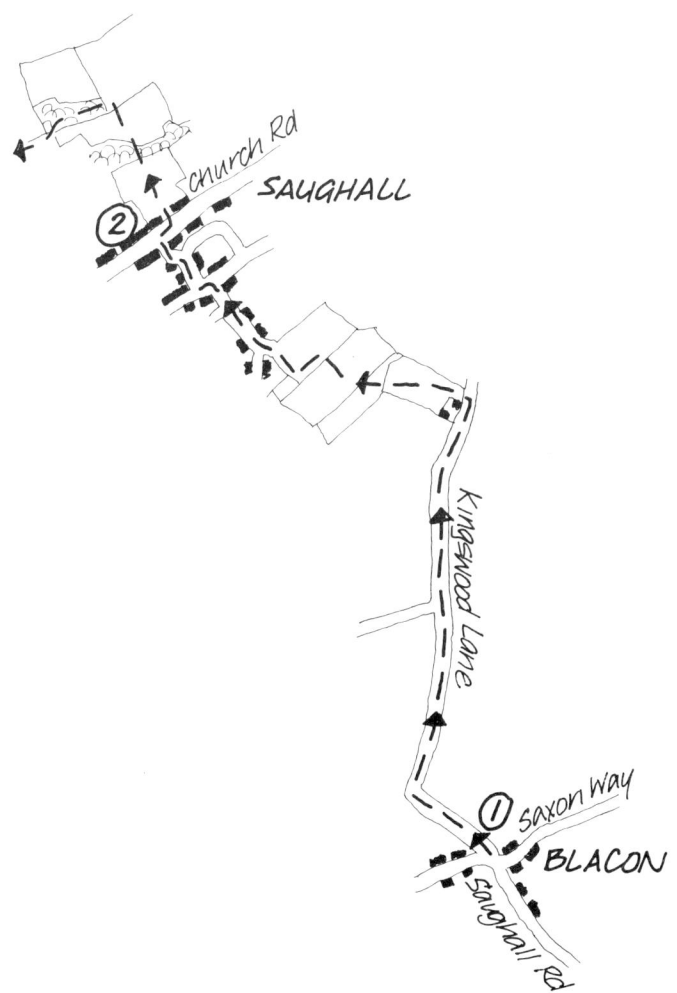

A Walker's Guide to the Wirral Shore Way

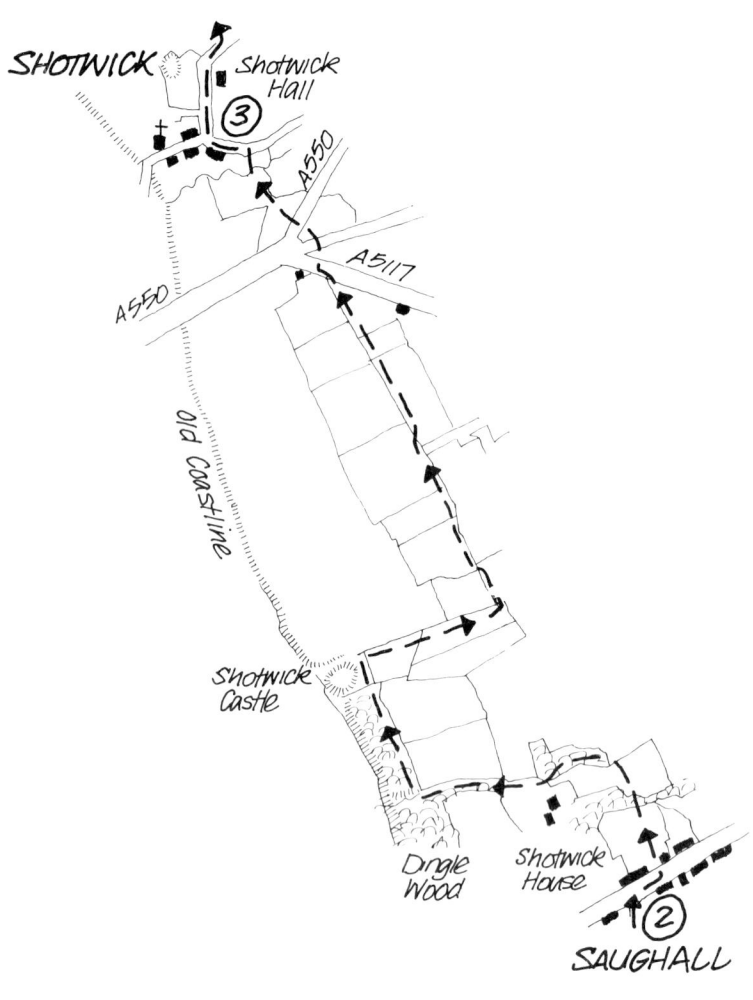

Its only claim to fame seems to be the unfortunate Mary Davies who was born here in the closing years of the sixteenth *century and came to be known as the "Horned Woman of Cheshire". The horns, which first appeared when she was 28 years old, were said to be like a "ram's horns" and "sadly grieved the old woman especially upon the change of weather". When she shed them, which happened every three to five years, they became prized curiosities and one is said to have been presented to the French King by an unnamed English Lord.*

2. Turn right and after about 40 yards cross the road where a sign indicates a footpath which passes between gardens before cutting through the centre of a large field. Beyond a belt of trees, continue straight ahead to a stile and footbridge over a stream. Bear left here and follow the "Permissive Footpath" through a small wood with a stream on the left.

This section of footpath has recently been opened to the public by Cheshire County Council and will eventually form part of a circular route taking in the site of Shotwick Castle.

Leave the woods by means of a footbridge on the left and continue beside the stream. At the bottom of the field bear right over a stile and, staying beside the stream, make your way into Dingle Wood. At a T junction above the steep coastal step, turn right, cross the stream by a footbridge and make your way up a flight of steps.

This steep slope marks the old coastline of Wirral before the Dee was diverted into the "New Cut" on the Welsh side of the river, allowing the vast reclamation schemes of the late eighteenth century. The name of nearby Sealand recalls these schemes.

Continue on the obvious footpath through the woods with fields on the right until you enter fields by the earthworks of Shotwick Castle, turning right after you have crossed the stile.

These earthworks, which stand on the edge of the old shoreline, are all that now remain of Shotwick Castle, built to defend the English-Welsh border during the early medieval period. Remnants of the stone walls, which stood until the seventeenth century, have all been removed now and probably found their way into local buildings.

The castle is thought to have been built by Hugh Lupus, Earl of Chester and later used by the English kings during their wars with the Welsh and Irish in the twelfth and thirteenth centuries. Henry II led an army against Wales in 1156 from Wirral and probably retreated to Shotwick eleven years later following his defeat on the Berwyn Mountains. In the following century both Henry III and Edward I passed through Shotwick on their way to conquests in Wales and Ireland and almost certainly stayed at the castle.

By the early fourteenth century the death of Prince Llewellyn led to peace with the Welsh and the castle was allowed to fall into ruins.

Continue beside the earthworks and turn right over a stile following the path along field edges once more. At a signpost ("Public Footpath") turn left and follow the footpath along field edges to the busy A5117. Take care not to miss a stile and footbridge on the right about half way along the path where a change is made to the right-hand side of the hedge.

Cross the road opposite farm buildings and look for a stile behind the large road sign. Cut through a small field to a stile and lane. Turn left here then immediately right over a stile (signposted "Shotwick") and cut through a second small field (keeping left) to a stile which leads through metal railings to the A550. Opposite, a stile and sign indicate the continuation of the field path to "Shotwick". Continue straight through the field (aiming to the right of the church tower) and turn right through a gate in the corner. Immediately on the left, a second gate leads into a sloping field, descend the field to a footbridge over a stream and rise to Shotwick Lane. Turn left now and follow the lane to Shotwick Church.

This quiet hamlet, now by-passed by traffic on the busy Welsh road lies almost forgotten, yet for centuries it stood on the the main route from Wirral to North Wales. Before the River Dee around Sealand was reclaimed, a tidal road ran from the lane beside the church to Flint in North Wales.

Earlier still an anchorage was built at Shotwick as a replacement for Chester, then suffering the effects of siltation. During the Middle Ages several armies sailed from here to battles in Ireland and North Wales, among them the famous Wirral archers who practiced their skills in the fields below the church. In later years anchorages were established at Burton, Neston and Parkgate as siltation of the river continued.

Today the swirling waters of the River Dee have become dry land, even the wild marshes have disappeared. In their place lie fields, hedges, cattle and sheep, and in more recent years, the monstrous buildings of the steel industry at Shotton. The only clue to earlier events is the nearby coastal step below the church and the almost artificially flat land between here and North Wales.

With the tidal road across the marshes no longer in use Shotwick lies frozen in time. Most of the attractive old buildings date from the seventeenth century although one of the oldest is probably Greyhound Farm, previously the Greyhound Inn. It was here in 1750 that three Irish labourers were arrested for beating and killing a fellow traveller on the nearby Chester Road. They were detained over night at Shotwick before being sent to jail at Chester Castle the next day. Two were found guilty, hanged at Boughton and their bodies "hung up in irons near Two Mills on the Heath, in the road to Parkgate". Today Gibbet Mill, which was built shortly after, marks the spot where they hung.

Chapter 2
Shotwick - Parkgate
Distance 6 miles

3. Retrace your steps from the church and turn left into the cul-de-sac leading to Shotwick Hall.

The hall was built in 1662 in the late Elizabethan style by Joseph Hockenhull as a replacement for the ancient manor house. In the fields to the left, a tree covered mound surrounded by the remnants of a moat are all that remain of the ancient building. The Hockenhulls held Shotwick from the time of Edward I.

Beyond the hall turn left onto a track signposted, "Puddington". Follow the track to a gate and continue along the field edges. After the third gate turn right along the field edge, then bear diagonally left through the centre of the field. Pass to the left of a pond and aim for the corner of the field with a house on the right and a farm on the left. Bear left along the field edge then cut through the centre of the field to a farm track. Turn left here and follow the lane to a T junction.

Turn left and continue a short distance to Puddington. As you enter the village turn left between houses (indicated by a footpath sign) and follow the path, first along a short access road, then bear right onto an enclosed footpath with Puddington Old Hall to your left. At the road continue straight ahead beside the barn (sign) and join a farm track. Follow the track to Puddington Lane.

The hall, built in 1490 has been greatly altered over the centuries and as a result little of the original building remains, although traces of the moat can still be seen. Of particular note are the remains of a dovecote built at a time when fresh winter meat was hard to come by. The keeping of pigeons in this way was a guarded privilege among the gentry and this dovecote is one of only two in Wirral, the other being at Gayton.

For over 500 years the manor was held by the Massey family, famed for their love of battle. Various members of this ancient family distinguished themselves fighting on both foreign and English soil. A tale of particular note concerns

Shotwick Church

A Walker's Guide to the Wirral Shore Way

William Massey, who, in 1715 at the age of 60 joined the Pretenders forces at Preston. When they were overwhelmed by

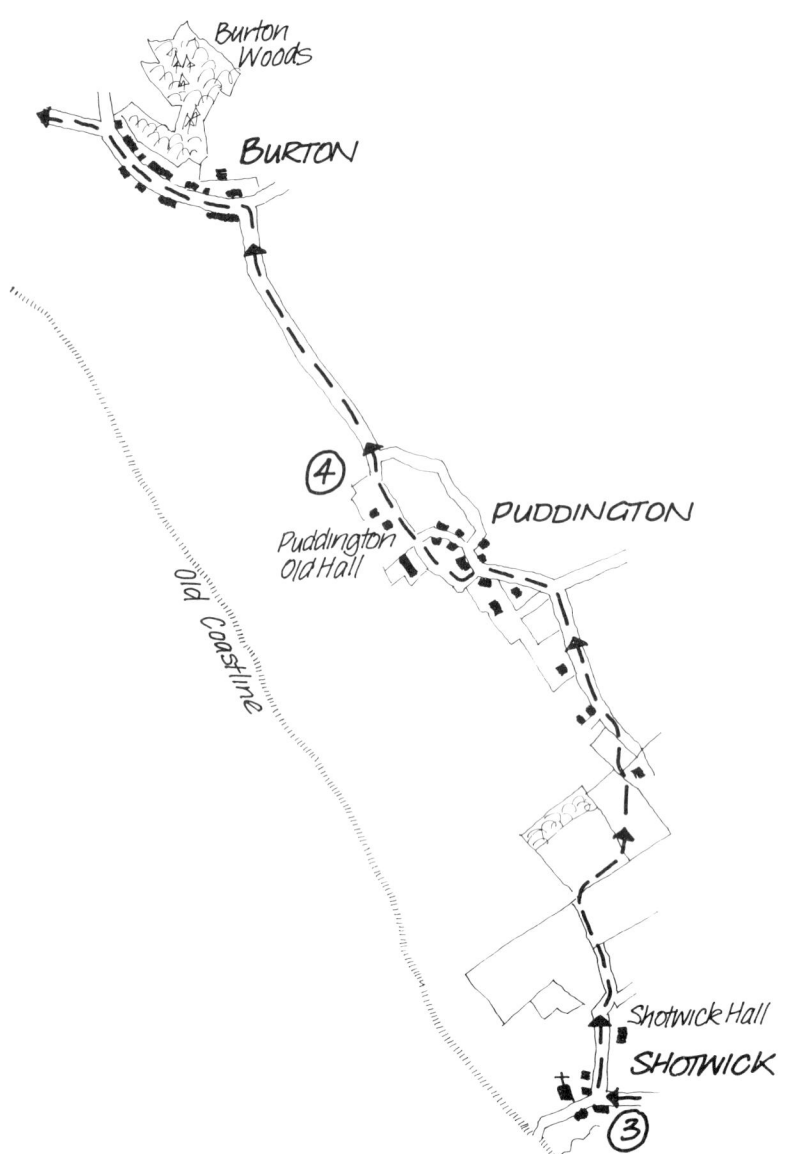

Royalists and surrendered William fled to Puddington. He rode none stop to Speke where he forced his exhausted steed across the Mersey almost at its widest point, gaining the far bank near Hooton. On reaching the hall the beast collapsed and died and was buried where it fell.

William knew that home was not a safe haven however and that he would soon be arrested and face execution. In a bid to create an alibi he had thrashed a local farmer on his return to the hall and, knowing that he would be summoned to court, used this, along with his speedy return to prove that he could not have been in Preston on the day of the battle. This, it seems did not help him, he was arrested shortly after and died in prison at Chester Castle in February 1716.

4. Bear left at Puddington Lane and continue to Burton turning left into the village.

This is one of the most attractive villages in Wirral and the impression given is that it has remained as a sleepy undisturbed back water for centuries. In fact, this is far from the truth. Like many villages along this coast, it enjoyed a brief period of prosperity as a seaport and has seen the busy movement of both exotic foreign goods and large armies through its main street.

Burton took over from Shotwick as a port when the River Dee began to silt up towards the end of the thirteenth century. Burton Point, which protrudes into the estuary below the village, provided an ideal location for an anchorage offering shelter from northwesterly gales. It was from here that Cheshire archers sailed to Ireland to fight for Richard II in the fourteenth century. By the middle of the following century it had developed into an international port handling goods from as far away as Spain. By this time its days were numbered however, and within a hundred years the New Quay had been built at Neston as the river became too shallow for larger vessels.

Today Burton Point is surrounded by farmland and lies beyond the reach of even the highest tides. Of the one-time port there is no sign, although there are earthworks here, possibly of Saxon origin which may have given Burton its name (from the Saxon "burh" meaning stronghold or fortified place and "tun" meaning farmstead or village).

Barn End, Burton

As you leave Burton bear left into Station Road and follow the lane down to the old shoreline at Denhall.

Here at last you begin to sense that the sea is not too distant, that the vast treeless expanse before you is not completely dry land. The old coastline is clearly visible now and there are even pockets of sand here and there recalling the fine sandy beaches of earlier years. Although there is a feeling of deterioration, as if the best has been and gone, the marshes are far from lifeless and offer a valuable habitat of national importance to the many species of wildfowl which winter here each year. In 1979, 5,000 acres of Burton Marsh were purchased from the British Steel Corporation by the R.S.P.B to ensure its future conservation.

5. Where the lane turns sharp right continue straight ahead along the marsh edge for about one mile, signposted "Public Footpath Quayside 1".

Just before the Harp Inn you will see the remains of Denhall Quay on the left, one of the many relics from Wirral's maritime past. It was used primarily to ship coal, brought from the nearby Wirral Colliery, to Ireland until the channel became too shallow for boats to dock here. The quay is quite well preserved and many of the large stone blocks are still in place.

Further along the coast lie the spoil heaps of the Wirral Colliery which closed in 1928 after operating for 175 years. Here men and boys toiled in wet and dirty conditions to bring poor quality coal to the surface from almost two miles beneath the estuary. The mines were so plagued by water, which seeped through the porous sandstone, that coal was transported along "canals" or partly flooded shafts in small boats before being hauled to the surface by hand.

The path continues along the marsh edge to the remains of the Old Quay, once an important sea port.

A Walker's Guide to the Wirral Shore Way

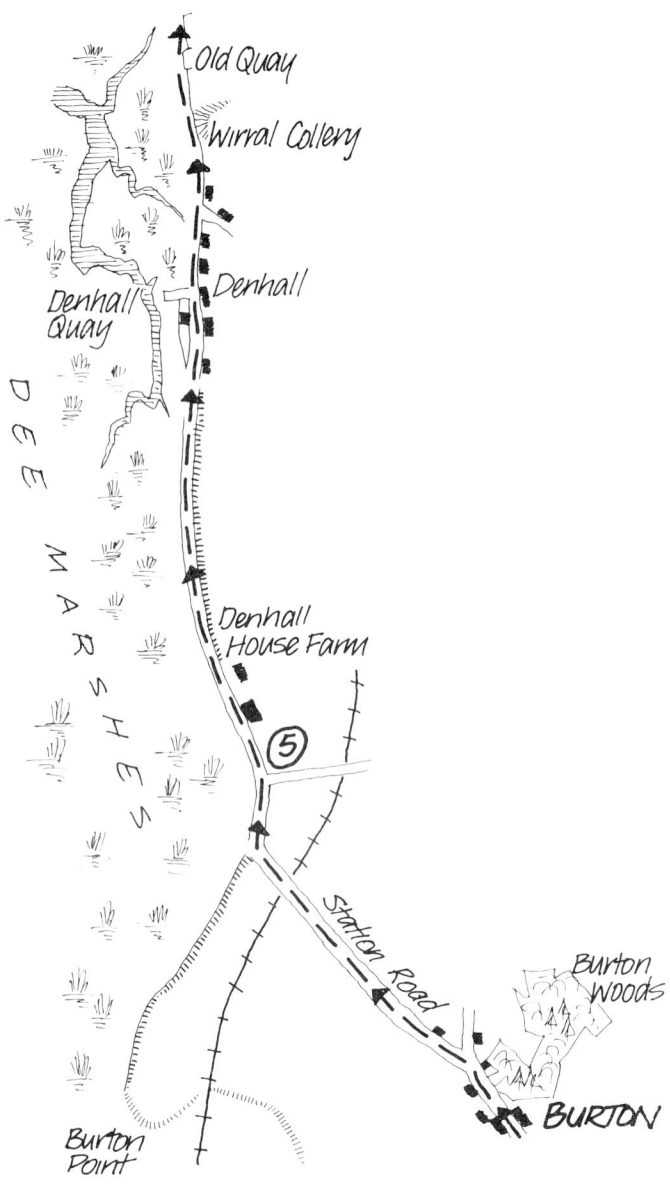

Note: Between Marshlands Road and the Old Quay there is no public right of way although the path along the marsh edge is well walked and there appears to be no access problem. Should the situation change, walkers are reminded that they have no legal right to walk here, the land owners wishes should therefore be respected.

As we have already learned the Port of Chester began to lose its sea trade in the thirteenth century because of "the abundance of sands which had choked the creek". As a result, anchorages had been established down stream at Burton and Shotwick, but by the sixteenth century these too had become choked. The "New Quay", as it was then called, was built beside the deep channel at Neston around 1550 and enjoyed a brief period of prosperity before it too was replaced by a new port at Parkgate. From then on it became known as the "Old Quay" and gradually fell into ruins.

Beyond the Old Quay continue along the marsh edge for about half a mile before bearing right by bungalows. Turn left into Manorial Road and at the end of the road join a short footpath signposted, "Public Footpath The Parade 1/4". This leads to a rough access road, continue straight ahead here and, where the road bears right, turn left onto a narrow footpath which leads to the marsh edge once more. Turn right now and continue along Parkgate's old sea front (The Parade).

Chapter 3
Parkgate - Thurstaston Common
Distance 5 1/2 miles

It is over half a century since the sea finally abandoned Parkgate leaving the attractive cottages to look out onto acres of marsh grass instead of bright yellow sand. It is perhaps hard to imagine when we look out onto these marshes just how much this landscape has changed in the last three centuries.

In its hey-day Parkgate was a bustling sea port of national importance. This was partly due to the Dublin Packet service which ran on a demand basis for over 70 years with many famous passengers, among them Handel and John Wesley, making the sometimes hazardous crossing.

Parkgate eventually lost this trade to Holyhead where a shorter and more reliable crossing could be obtained. This was due in part to the improved road travel through North

Parkgate at the turn of the century

A Walker's Guide to the Wirral Shore Way

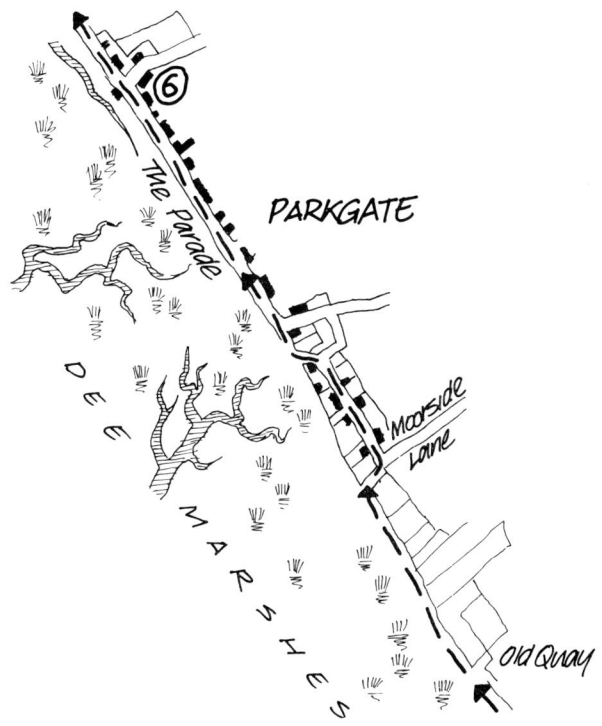

Wales, along with the rapid silting of the River Dee which robbed Parkgate of its navigable water. The last boat to land passengers here was in 1811.

This was not the end of Parkgate's prosperity however. The sands which had clogged the channel now attracted a new kind of visitor, the sea bather. Throughout the early decades of the nineteenth century Parkgate was "much resorted to by the gay and fashionable world". The coming of the railways in later years took many of these visitors to other resorts but locals continued to bathe here until the 1940s when the marsh finally reached the sea wall.

Today you can barely see the sea from here, except on very rare occasions, however, we need only reflect on the fate of the more prosperous ports, such as Birkenhead and Liverpool, who inherited much of Parkgate's trade, to see what might have been.

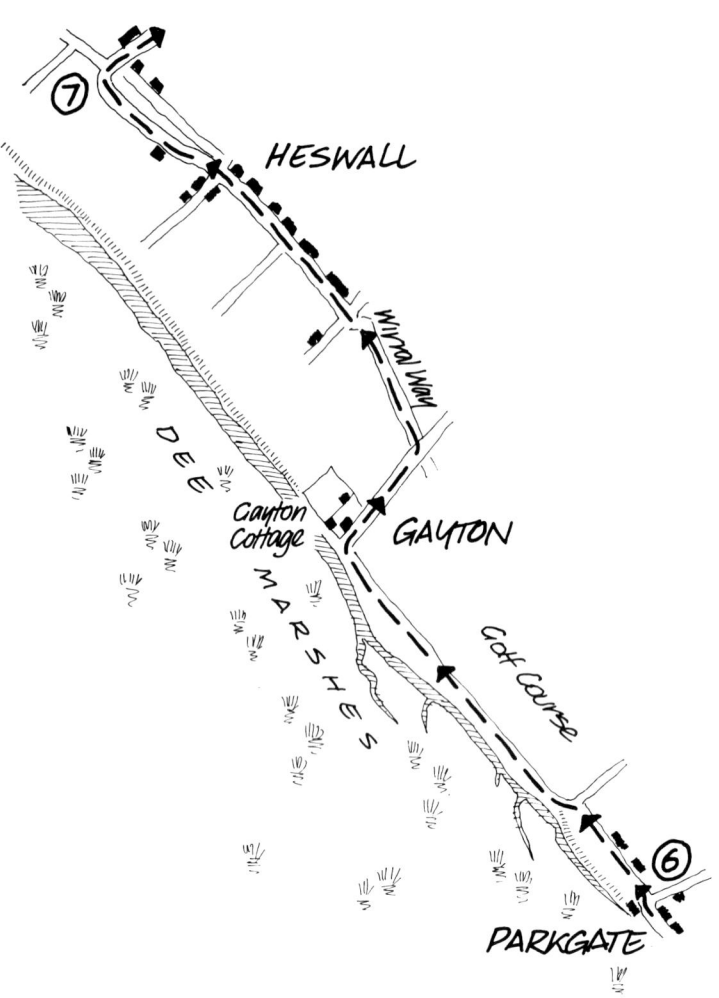

6. At the northern end of The Parade the road bears sharp right, continue straight ahead here to the Old Baths car park before following the footpath along the marsh edge to Gayton.

Like Parkgate the sea is a seldom visitor to the old shoreline here although for nearly 600 years a ferry regularly crossed the estuary to Flintshire. The last ferry house still stands and is now called Gayton Cottage.

Beyond Gayton there is no shoreline footpath so we must turn away from the marshes and join the Wirral Way for a while. Bear right into the lane then turn left onto the Wirral Way after 500 yards or so.

After a short stretch on the Wirral Way bear left by houses and at Riverbank Road turn right. Follow Riverbank Road, which shortly runs into Davenport Road and at the Wirral Country Park sign bear left into Wittering Lane.

7. At the end of the lane bear right over the Wirral Way and follow Delavor Road for about 200 yards, before turning left into Pipers Lane. Almost immediately, turn right into Bush Way and bear left into Heswall Dales Local Nature Reserve.

Follow the obvious bridleway marked with arrows and contained here and there by wooden fencing. Keep right at a fork and after some distance bear right onto a track by Dale Farm. Follow the track to Oldfield Road, turn left, and at a crossroad continue straight ahead to Oldfield Hall, now a farmhouse.

It was at this old manor house that Sir Rowland Stanley, one of the most celebrated Cheshire knights of Queen Elizabeth's reign, spent his remaining years. An inscription above the door reads "R 1604 S" indicating a ten year stay. He died in 1614 at the ripe old age of 96, quite an achievement, both for the period in which he lived and the occupation which he had chosen.

Keep to the right of the farm and follow the signed footpath which runs along the top of the hillside towards Thurstaston church.

Below us, the green marshes have at last been replaced by fine yellow sands giving an impression of what much of the estuary looked like until about 200 years ago. Within decades this too will have disappeared beneath the spreading green carpet which has made such rapid progress along this coast.

Although this is a natural process man gave nature a helping hand here when he diverted the River Dee into a canal over on the Welsh side of the estuary in the eighteenth century. This had the effect of forcing the main deep water channel (which enabled ports like Parkgate and Neston to take sea going vessels) over to the Welsh side, thus allowing sands along the Wirral coast to build up more rapidly. In addition, a particularly hardy and fast spreading species of marsh grass was introduced when the estuary around Sealand was reclaimed. This colonised the sands at a tremendous rate robbing resorts like Parkgate of its once famous beach.

At the lane continue straight ahead and take the first road on the right beyond the church. Turn left at the busy A540 and bear right onto Thurstaston Common just beyond the Cottage Loaf public house, signposted "Public Footpath to Royden Park". Follow the path to a small school and just beyond, turn sharp left onto a broad sandy path which rises to the top of Thurstaston Hill, highest point on the common.

At 255 feet, Thurstaston Hill is not the highest point in Wirral but it undoubtedly has one of the finest panoramas. A view finder near the highest point identifies major land marks along with distances and was erected in 1942 in memory of Andrew Blair, founder of Liverpool and District Ramblers Association. An inscription reads "For many years a keen worker for the preservation of cross country footpaths and amenities of the countryside. Author of several books for walkers."

A Walker's Guide to the Wirral Shore Way

The view on a clear day takes in much of Wirral and North Wales. Below us green fields sweep down from Thurstaston church to the marshes and shallow waters of the Dee Estuary, while the Clwyd Range stand proudly beyond. If you are lucky the higher peaks of Snowdonia and the Great Orme will just be visible.

Further north the wooded slopes of Caldy Hill act as a barrier to the urban sprawl of eastern Wirral. Fields and woods quickly give way to houses, factories, pylons and motorways. Beyond is the familiar Liverpool skyline dominated by its two cathedrals.

The whole of Thurstaston Common was purchased with remarkable foresight by Birkenhead Town Council as far back as 1879 for "the benefit of the neighbourhood" and "convenience of the inhabitants". Had this not been the case this bit of greenery may well have disappeared beneath the bricks and mortar of suburbia decades ago.

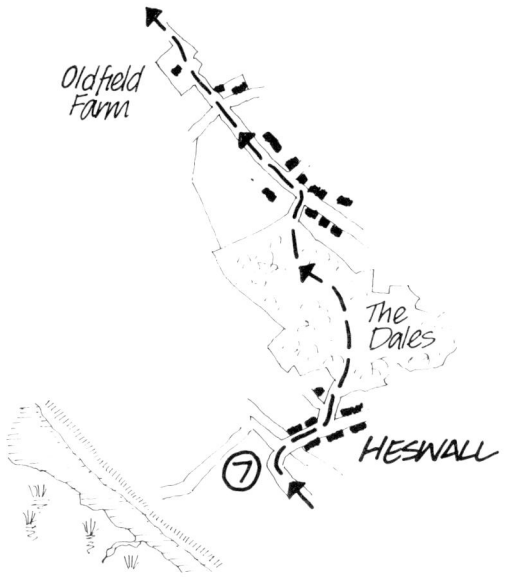

Chapter 4
Thurstaston Common - Hilbre Point
Distance 4 1/2 miles

8. From the triangulation pillar descend to the car park immediately below the summit and turn right onto the road. After about half a mile turn left into fields where a sign indicates the "Public Footpath to Caldy". Keep to the field edge turning right through a gate in the corner and after a second field join a wide track which cuts through a horse paddock towards Caldy.

At the road continue straight ahead (Long Hey Road) and after 150 yards, where the road bears left, continue on the enclosed footpath (sign, "Public Footpath to Stapleton Wood"). Turn left at the road and continue towards Caldy village.

Look for a footpath sign on the right ("Public Bridleway") beside Caldecot Cottage and follow the sandy footpath into the woods. At the road turn left and then right into Thorsway. After about 150 yards cross over and take the enclosed footpath between gardens on the left. Turn right in the woods and at a clearing bear half-left by wooden seats in the direction of two distant masts. Continue now on the obvious footpath to the column at Column Road.

This was erected in 1841 by the Trustees of Liverpool Docks as a beacon for river traffic and replaced a large windmill destroyed two years earlier by gales.

9. Turn left into Column Road and where the road bears left down the hill cross over and continue along Grange Old Road (beside Black House Hill). A well hidden footpath (sign "Public Footpath to Grange Hill") which joins the driveway to Grange Hill, a large house on the right, leads to the war memorial on the hill itself.

A Walker's Guide to the Wirral Shore Way

From the memorial continue northwards over the hill to Lang Lane and turn left. Follow the road to Redhouse Lane, a cul-de-sac on the right which eventually runs into a narrow footpath between gardens. At Orrysdale Road cross over and take a footpath on the left beside the school. Follow the path

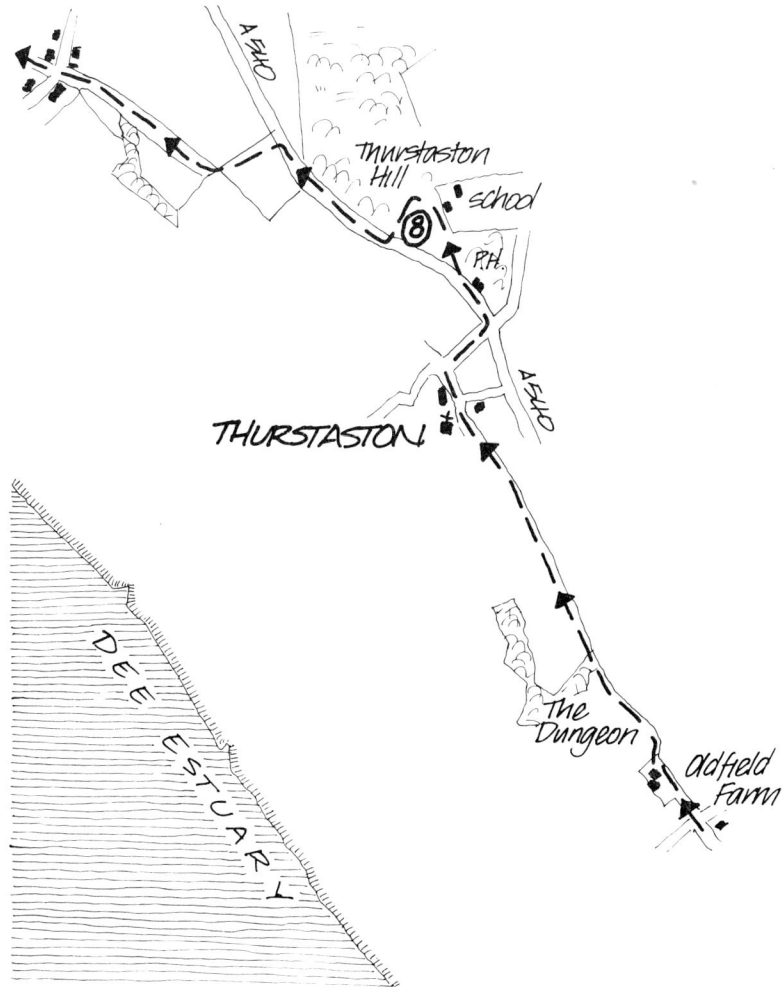

A Walker's Guide to the Wirral Shore Way

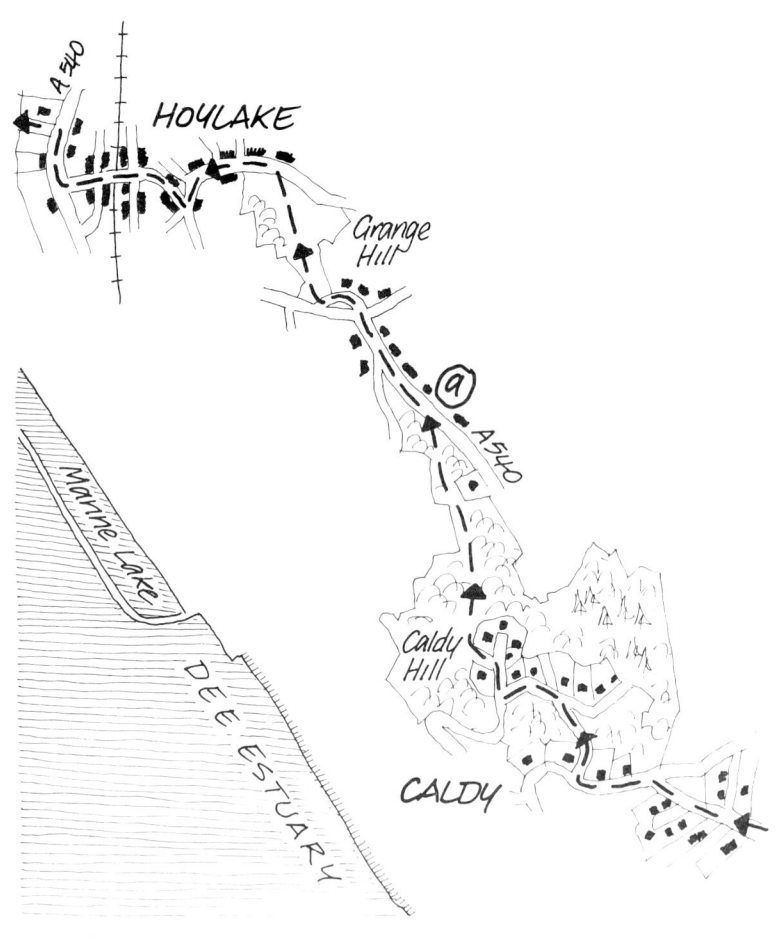

over the railway and straight across the following road onto a similar footpath. At the busy A540 (Meols Drive) turn right and after 300 yards bear left into Pinfold Lane. At the end of the lane continue straight across the golf course to the shoreline opposite the Hilbre Islands. Turn right now and either follow the sand or wooden walkway to Hilbre Point.

A Walker's Guide to the Wirral Shore Way

200 years ago this northern coast was a very different place, a line of shifting sand dunes battered by gales sheltered a handful of fishermen's cottages, yet evidence of some of Wirral's earliest settlements have been found here. The finds, which include coins, brooches, precious stones and pottery, cover a period of 1,700 years and date back to the Roman outpost at Meols. Many of the items were recovered from the famous "submerged forest" visible on the sand at low tide until about 60 years ago. The late Norman Ellison in his book The Wirral Peninsula *describes the forest in this way "The clean stretch of sand was broken by a black patch, perhaps a half-mile in length, which a closer inspection revealed to be a thick stratum of peat, brown twigs, leaves, mosses, ferns and lichens, all tightly compressed. Above this mass, a large number of tree trunks, perhaps three or four feet high, stood erect, whilst many fallen trunks and large branches lay partly buried."*

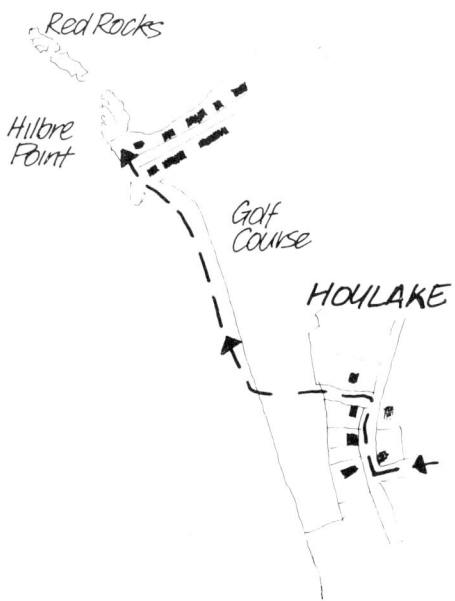

The origin of the forest is uncertain but it could well be a relic of Wirral's ancient woodland buried by the shifting sands before deforestation could take place. Certainly this part of Wirral has seen dramatic changes in the last 700 years. The sand flats at nearby Hoylake were once a deep water pool or lake, known as "Hoyle Lake", which existed until the canalisation of the Dee in the eighteenth century caused it to silt up.

It was referred to as the "Heyepol" during the reign of King John and was protected by a great sand bank which extended across the mouth of the estuary. It was used for centuries as a deep water anchorage and embarkation point by ships too large to reach Chester and it was from here that William III sailed to Ireland in 1690 to defeat James II at the battle of the Boyne. The previous year Duke Schomberg gathered a great army of almost 10,000 and sailed against James in 90 ships which gathered in Hoyle Lake.

When the lake finally disappeared it was replaced by a fine sandy beach which, during the late eighteenth century when sea bathing became fashionable, attracted a large host of pleasure seekers eager to sample this new found pastime. Today Hoylake still has its sandy beach though you will find no sign of Hoyle Lake or the submerged forest.

Across the sands to our left lie the Hilbre Islands, easily reached at low tide and once home to a seventh century hermit by the name of Hidleburgh. There is no record of who this lady was or even how long she lived here but her solitary life of prayer and penance inspired the setting up of a holy shrine which attracted pilgrims throughout the Middle Ages. She did leave us her name though, Hilbre means Hidleburgh's "ey" or island.

During this period Hilbre came under the ownership of the Abbey of Saint Werburgh's at Chester and monks in varying numbers lived on the island until the mid sixteenth century.

By this time life was far from quiet in this busy corner of Wirral. As we have already learned, ships often used the nearby Hoyle Lake as an anchorage and as they grew in numbers a customs house was built and officers stationed here. Hilbre is also mentioned as the embarkation point for thousands of Queen Elizabeth's troops sent to conquer Ireland in the sixteenth century.

There has even been a small amount of industry on Hilbre. In 1662 a certain Dr Leigh set up a salthouse for the production of salt using raw materials brought from the mid Cheshire salt fields at Northwich. There has also been a public house although its owners are reputed to have gathered more wealth through the activity of wrecking.

Today the visitor will find little evidence of these activities although a trip across the sands is well worth while and makes a fine alternative finish to the Wirral Shore Way. You can reach the islands from the slipway at the northern end of the Marine Lake, West Kirby, about two hours either side of low water (the tide surrounds the islands for four hours out of every twelve). Aim for Little Eye, the southern most and smallest island, then follow the sandstone reef to Middle Eye and finally Hilbre Island. Tide times can be obtained from Thurstaston Visitor Centre, by telephone on: 051 648 3884/ 4371 and are displayed at the Marine Lake.

Acknowledgements

Special thanks are due to Cheshire County Council's Countryside Managements Service who have agreed to maintain and way-mark all public rights of way within Cheshire used by the *Wirral Shore Way*.

Mara Publications

If you enjoyed your walk along the *Wirral Shore Way* why not try one of our other walking guides. These are available from bookshops or direct from the publisher. Please check prices by telephone before ordering.

Walking in Wirral

Circular Walks along the Sandstone Trail

Walking on the Clwyd Hills and the Vale of Llangollen

Mara Publications
22 Crosland Terrace, Helsby, Warrington, Cheshire. WA6 9LY.
Telephone: (0928) 723744.